Rosemary Hellyer-Jones

Barker's World

Ernst Klett Verlag
Stuttgart · Leipzig

Contents

Before you read

- *Do you like dogs?*
- *Is there a dog in your family? If not, would you like to have a dog?*

> Yes! I think dogs are great, because …

> No! I think dogs are a pain, because …

- *How can you make a happy home for a dog?*

> It's a good idea to …

> It's important to … with your dog.

German Shepherd

lead

bowl of dog food

dog bed

collar

Jack Russell Terrier

Yorkshire Terrier

rubber bone / toys

lead [liːd] Leine • **bowl** [bəʊ] Napf • **dog food** [ˈdɒg fuːd] Hundefutter • **collar** [ˈkɒlə] Halsband • **rubber bone** [ˌrʌbəˈbəʊnl] Gummiknochen • **toy** [tɔɪ] Spielzeug

Barker and his family

Here I am!

And here are my pets!

Richard Taylor

Sue Taylor

Jade Taylor

Lisa Taylor

Ben Taylor

1 Hello!

Woof! Hello, everybody! I'm Barker. You know, I live in Greenwich. My house is in Pond Road. It's a very nice house – I love it! And I've got a garden, too. That's great. I'm four years old now – and I'm a really big dog. I'm the
5 boss here, anyway.

Do you know my pets? Let me tell you about them. First, there's Lisa. She's my favourite pet. She usually does what I want. That's good, of course. She sleeps in my room upstairs. There's only one bed, but it's nice and big. I sleep
10 on it, of course, but Lisa sleeps in it. That's because she often feels cold. And no wonder! She hasn't got a nice warm coat like I've got.

I've got another bed downstairs. In the kitchen. I sometimes sleep there in the day time. It's only a small
15 bed. Too small for Lisa, of course. But it's just right for me, and there's room in it for all my toys. I like it a lot.

Then there's Ben. He's sixteen. (Lisa is eleven.) He's a nice pet, too, but he hasn't always got time for me. He only does what he wants. Not like Lisa. When I go to the park,
20 she always comes with me. That girl really understands me.

Jade is my pet, too. She's only five. (That's very young for a pet!) I like her a lot, because she sometimes gives me my food. But Lisa is still my favourite – there's nobody like
25 her. Nobody!

I've got two old pets, too. Sue Taylor – that's Lisa's mother – and Richard, her father. I call them Mum and Dad, but they aren't my parents, of course. I don't need parents.

Sometimes parents can be really silly. Mum, for
30 example. She has got some very silly ideas. She thinks my bed upstairs is only for Lisa. She sometimes finds me on

---

2 pond [pɒnd] Teich • **4 really** ['rɪəli] wirklich • **5 anyway** ['eniweɪ] sowieso, jedenfalls • **11 No wonder!** [nəʊ 'wʌndə] Kein Wunder! • **12 coat** [kəʊt] *hier:* Fell • **15 just** [dʒʌst] *hier:* gerade • **20 to understand** [ˌʌndə'stænd] verstehen

it, and then she gets angry. I've got no idea why! After all, I never sleep on her bed. (There isn't room for me on it, anyway. Dad is so big!)

Dad has got some silly ideas, too. At dinner time, for example. And at breakfast. Lisa knows I like ham and 5 cheese, and things like that. So she often leaves something on her plate for me. Then she gives it to me in the kitchen. But Dad doesn't like that. I don't know why. Where's the problem? After all, I lick the plate OK, so they really needn't wash it up. But my pets like extra work. They wash 10 up all the plates, and sometimes they really aren't dirty. Sometimes I sit there and watch them. And I think: "How silly pets can be!"

Now, let me tell you something about my day.

2 In the mornings

My day always starts early. I'm usually awake at six o'clock. 15 That's too early for Lisa, of course. When I'm awake, I go downstairs. (Lisa always leaves the bedroom door open, so I can go in and out.) I go to the kitchen and have a drink of water. Sometimes I find one or two old dog biscuits in my bed, so I have them, too. I can't go out in the garden 20 yet, because the doors are still locked. So I go back upstairs and sleep again.

Lisa is usually still asleep at seven. But at 7.30 I wake her up. I lick her face and she says hello to me. Then she goes to the bathroom. I don't go in with her. I don't like 25 bathrooms! It's a very small bathroom, anyway, so there isn't much room for two.

---

1 **to get** [gɛt] werden • 1 **after all** [ˌɑːftər ˈɔːl] schließlich • 6 **to leave** [liːv] lassen • 7 **plate** [pleɪt] Teller • 9 **to lick** [lɪk] lecken • 10 **to wash up** [wɒʃ ˈʌp] abwaschen • 15 **awake** [əˈweɪk] wach • 18 **to have sth** [hæv] *hier:* etw. essen/trinken • 19 **dog biscuit** [ˈdɒɡˌbɪskɪt] Hundekuchen • 21 **locked** [lɒkt] abgeschlossen

When Lisa is in the bathroom, I go to Ben's room and wake him up. I always lick his face, too, so it's nice and clean. But when he gets up, he washes it again. Just like Lisa. How silly! I can't understand it.

5   I take Lisa downstairs with me. Mum and Dad are usually in the kitchen with Jade. Before breakfast Lisa takes me out. There isn't time for a walk now, so I just go into the garden. Lisa leaves me outside, and calls me in again when breakfast is ready. Sometimes that awful cat, Tiger
10 Jackson, is in our garden. Tiger lives in Hither Farm Road with Terry Jackson and his parents. The three pets are OK, but I don't like Tiger. Cats are silly animals, anyway. They go into people's gardens without permission. And they like to start fights, too! But not with really big dogs. They
15 never start a fight with me, anyway! When I see a cat in my garden, I bark a lot. I've got a very loud bark, you see. That scares cats, and they run away. So Tiger never stays in the garden long.

Well, nobody has got much time for me at breakfast.
20 Lisa gives me my biscuits. And sometimes there's a little bit of something for me on her plate. But nobody sits at the table long. Lisa and Ben leave the house with big bags. I don't know where they go. It's a puzzle.

Anyway, they've always got books and pencils and
25 things like that in their bags. Sometimes things to eat, too. You know – things like sandwiches or an apple. I always bark when they leave the house. I want to go with them, you see. But I can't! I sometimes run after Lisa, but she always stops me.

30 A few minutes later, Dad leaves the house with little Jade. Jade always waves and says, "Bye, Barker!" And then they're off – sometimes on their bikes.

---

3 clean [kli:n] sauber • **3 just like** [dʒʌst laɪk] genau wie • **6 to take sb out** [ˌteɪk sʌmbədi 'aʊt] jmdn. nach draußen bringen, ausführen • **13 without permission** [pə'mɪʃn] ohne Erlaubnis • **21 a bit** [ə bɪt] ein bisschen • **28 to run after sb** [rʌn 'ɑ:ftə sʌmbədi] jmdm. hinterherlaufen • **32 to be off** [bi: 'ɒf] weggehen

Soon it's time for Mum and me to leave the house. We go to the Jazz Café together. That's in Stockwell Street, so we always go by car. Mum drives, and I sit on the back seat.

The Jazz Café is great! It's Mum's café really, but I'm a great help. I usually sit at one of the windows, near the door. When people stop outside and look in the window, I'm always very friendly. I look at them and wag my tail. Then they usually come in.

When people are in the café, I'm very nice to them. And very polite! I don't bark or jump up, of course. Some people don't like that. But I make a very friendly face. Then they usually say hello and pat me on the head. I like that! Then I take them to Mum, and she shows them where they can sit. Mum brings them what they want to eat and drink. So I can go back to my place at the window and wait for the next customers.

1 **soon** [suːn] bald • 3 **back seat** [ˌbæk ˈsiːt] Rücksitz • 7 **to wag** [wæg] wedeln • 7 **tail** [teɪl] Schwanz • 10 **to jump up** [dʒʌmp ˈʌp] hochspringen • 12 **to pat** [pæt] tätscheln

I've got a bed in a small room near the kitchen, but I don't use it much. My job is too important for that, you see. And I love it!

But there's one silly thing. Really silly! The kitchen at
5 the café is a 'no-no'. (That means I can't go in. Don't ask me why!) Anyway, Mum and her helper, Sally, make all the food in the kitchen. Sandwiches and snacks, and things like that. And they make the drinks there, of course. Tea and coffee and hot chocolate, and lots of different cold
10 drinks, too. There's only water for me! And maybe a dog biscuit or two in my bed at lunchtime. Oh well, never mind. I haven't really got time for food, anyway. I'm so busy with my work in the café, you see.

3   Later in the day

The Jazz Café always closes at 5pm. So Mum and I get
15 back to Pond Road late in the afternoon. Lisa and Ben are usually at home again then. They are often very busy with their books and pens and things. That's boring for me, of course. So I usually sit near Lisa's chair. I look at her all the time. If she takes no notice, I bark a bit. That always helps!
20 She feels sorry for me then, you see.

"OK, Barker," she usually says. "Just five more minutes, OK?"

After a minute or two, I go into the hall and get my lead. When Lisa sees the lead on the floor near her chair, she
25 understands. Five minutes later, we are in the park!

The evening is my favourite time. All my pets are at home, and I feel happy after my walk. Hungry, too! Lisa gets my food ready, and I watch her. I usually have 'Bark-a-Lot'! It's great! Mum buys it for me, but Lisa always puts

---

11 **Never mind.** [ˌnevə ˈmaɪnd] Macht nichts. • 19 **if** [ɪf] wenn, falls • 19 **to take no notice** [teɪk nəʊ ˈnəʊtɪs] nicht reagieren • 20 **to feel sorry for sb** [ˌfiːl ˈsɒri fə sʌmbədi] Mitleid mit jmdm. haben • 23 **to get** [get] *hier:* holen • 24 **floor** [flɔː] Fußboden

it in my bowl. And I bark a lot, of course, when she opens the tin. There's 'Chicken Bark-a-Lot' and 'Beef Bark-a-Lot'. They both taste good, but 'Beef Bark-a-Lot' is my favourite. And no wonder! Nine out of ten dogs like it best. I know that from TV. 5

At our house, the evening is TV time. I think TV is boring, really. No real people or animals. Only pictures of them! And no smells! But my pets like TV. When they're all sitting on the sofa, we sometimes play a game. It's great fun! It goes like this: 10

I sit in front of the TV, and then they throw things at me. You know – shoes – or comics – or maybe a pencil or a bit of popcorn. Then I pick the things up and take them upstairs. (Not the popcorn, of course. I eat that!) If Lisa's door is open, I put the things in her room. If not, I leave 15 them in the old pets' bedroom – or in the bathroom.

Lisa is usually in bed at nine o'clock. I'm always downstairs then, in the kitchen. I wait there in my little bed. But when the old pets are in bed, I go upstairs, too. If Lisa is still awake, she strokes me. After that, I wash her 20 face a bit again. Then she pats me on the head and says good night.

A few minutes later I fall asleep – and another day is over.

4   A picnic – and a new friend

Woof! Here I am again! It's Sunday today. I love Sundays, 25 because my pets have got more time for me. The Jazz Café is open, but Mum and I don't go there on Sundays. Sally and her sister do all the work without us. So I often take all my pets out in our car.

2 **tin** [tɪn] Dose • 2 **beef** [biːf] Rindfleisch • 3 **to taste** [teɪst] schmecken •
8 **smell** [smel] Geruch, Duft • 11 **in front of** [ɪn 'frʌnt əv] vor • 13 **to pick sth up**
[ˌpɪk sʌmθɪŋ 'ʌp] etw. aufheben • 20 **to stroke** [strəʊk] streicheln

I like these trips a lot! Mum usually drives, and Dad reads the map. Lisa, Ben and Jade sit on the back seat. So there isn't much room for me. But I like it anyway – it's great to be all together!

5 I like to look out of the window. There are always lots of cars on the roads. And of course, sometimes there are dogs in the other cars! If it's a hot day, people often open their windows. So when I see other dogs, I can bark at them. They hear me and bark back. That's always great!

10 Well, today we're out in the country. It's like a big park here. Very quiet, with lots of big old trees. Great for walks! And I'm really excited, because we've got picnic things with us today. My pets are getting everything ready. Dad is getting the drinks out of the car, and Mum is putting the 15 tablecloth on the grass. Mm! That means it's lunchtime. Yes! Now she's putting the picnic things out! Let's just see what there is … Ah! Ham sandwiches! I love ham …

"No, Barker! Bad dog! Those are not for you!"

I know that, of course. But really, Mum always sees 20 everything! I don't know how she does it. I sometimes think she's got eyes in the back of her head.

Oh well, I can go and see what Lisa is doing.

She and Jade are by the stream. Jade is looking in the water.

25 "Hey, look, Lisa! There's a great big fish over there. Maybe we can catch it. Then we can have it for lunch. Let's ask Dad …"

Fish! That's a great idea. I like fish … Mm!

"But we can't catch fish here, Jade. We haven't got 30 permission … – Hey, Barker! What are you doing, you silly dog?"

Help!!! The water is cold! Like ice! Oh! What *am* I doing here? Oh, of course, that big fish … But where is it? How silly – I can't see it now. It isn't here …

---

5 out of ['aʊt əv] aus • **10 in the country** [ɪn ðə 'kʌntri] auf dem Land • **15 tablecloth** ['teɪblklɒθ] Tischdecke • **23 by the stream** [baɪ ðə 'striːm] am Bach • **26 to catch** [kætʃ] fangen

"Barker! Come out! Come out right now!"

That's Lisa's voice again. But I'm not listening. I don't want to listen. The water is really cold, but I like it now! And wow! The water here is deep, so I can swim! Yes! If I move my legs and keep my head up, I really can swim! ⁵

This is great. Watch me, everybody! Watch!

"Hey, Barker, stop it now! Come here! Oh, look, Jade! Ben! He's swimming to the other side. Barker, come back!"

But I don't want to come back. I'm on the other side now – and it's nice here. Great! There are lots of big trees, and – ¹⁰ hey, what's that? A rabbit! "Woof!! Woof!!"

"Oh, look!" It's Jade's voice this time. "Look, Lisa, he's chasing a rabbit now!"

• • •

2 **voice** [vɔɪs] Stimme • 4 **deep** [diːp] tief • 5 **to move** [muːv] bewegen • 5 **leg** [leg] Bein • 5 **to keep sth up** [ˌkiːp sʌmθɪŋ ˈʌp] etw. hoch halten • 8 **side** [saɪd] Seite • 11 **rabbit** [ˈræbɪt] Kaninchen

Yuk! I've got sand in my nose. And in my mouth, too. And it tastes awful! That's the big problem with rabbits. They live in holes. And I'm a big dog. So I can't get down those silly little holes. Ah, well! Never mind. Maybe Lisa has got
5 a sandwich for me. But first I must swim back through that stream … OK then, everybody, here I come!

• • •

"Help! What's this? Oh no, it's Barker!"
10   "Hey, stop that, Barker! You're making us all wet!"
   "Not on the tablecloth, Barker! You're wet and dirty! Bad dog!"
   "We don't want a shower, you silly dog! Go away!"
   How can pets be so silly? Just a bit of water, and they
15 get angry! First Lisa and Ben. Then Mum and Dad. I can't understand it. They like showers in the bathroom. (Dad even sings in the shower!) So why not here? It's a puzzle.

• • •

These trips are always over too soon! Now we're in the car again. It's time to go back home. My coat is still a bit wet.
20 Nobody wants me on the back seat now. So I'm sitting on the floor.

• • •

We're back, and I'm jumping down from the car. I feel excited, but I don't know why. I just know – something is different. There's a new smell!
25   "Hey, Barker!" That's Ben. "We've got new neighbours. Come and say hello!"
   New neighbours! So that's it.
   Now they're talking to my pets over the garden fence. I want to see who they are, of course. – Now I'm at the fence,
30 too. I'm wagging my tail.

---

1 **Yuk!** [jʌk] Igitt! • 1 **nose** [nəʊz] Nase, Schnauze • 1 **mouth** [maʊθ] Mund, *hier:* Maul • 3 **hole** [həʊl] Loch • 13 **shower** [ʃaʊə] Dusche • 25 **neighbour** [ˈneɪbə] Nachbar • 28 **fence** [fɛns] Zaun

14

"Woof!"

"Hello, Barker! You remember me, right? Well, I live here now – with my mum."

Oh, it's Jack Davidson! I know him from the park. He's one of Ben's friends. He's really nice. He always talks to me when he sees me in the park with Ben or Lisa. I like that, of course! Lots of people take no notice of dogs. They only say hello to other people. Sometimes I think they don't even see us dogs! How silly.

"Hey, where's Sherry?" Jack is talking to his mum.

"In the kitchen, I think. Wait a minute." Now she's going into their house. What is she doing? – Ah, here she is again. And … what's this?

"Woof! Woof! Woof!!"

I can't believe my eyes. There's a dog with her! Yes!

A beautiful Golden Labrador – just like me!

"This is Sherry, our new dog. Say hello to everybody, Sherry!"

Well, this is a surprise! For my pets, too. Another Labrador in Pond Road! Next door, even!

Jack's mum is explaining. "We've got Sherry from my parents. She's their dog really. But they want to sell their house – and buy a small flat. So Sherry is with us now. It's great for her here, of course – with this big garden!"

And it's great for me, too. Sherry is looking at me through the fence and she's wagging her tail already!

5   A day by the sea

Guess where I am today! – I'm on the beach. Yes! With all my pets, of course. It's a sunny day, nice and warm. They all like to be by the sea – and I like it, too. We've got picnic

---

16 **Golden Labrador** [ˌɡəʊldn ˈlæbrədɔː] *Hunderasse* • 20 **next door** [nekstˈdɔː] nebenan • 26 **already** [ɔːˈlredi] schon • 27 **beach** [biːtʃ] Strand

things for lunch again, and there's no table, of course. Just right for me!

But it isn't lunchtime yet. So, what are my pets doing? Ah! Ben is swimming in the sea. Jade is building a sandcastle.
5 Dad is helping her. Lisa is reading a magazine. And Mum is just lying there in the sun. Nobody wants to play.

Oh well, never mind. It's a big beach. And there are lots of people here today. I can go and look for things to do … And I must say, it's sometimes nice *without* my pets for a
10 bit.

This is great! I'm running by the sea – where the little waves come in over the sand. It's fun to feel the cold water on my legs.

"Woof! Woof!"
15 Oh! Another dog! But where?? I must go and look. Over there, maybe? By the beach huts? Let's see …

• • •

I like it up here, anyway. There's a nice little beach café here. Eddie, the ice cream man, is my friend. There he is! He's selling ice creams to some people in front of me.
20 A woman and a boy. I must go over and say hello to Eddie.

"Woof!" It's my turn now. And wow, I'm hungry!

"Hello, Barker!" That's Eddie. He knows my name. "Here without your people today?" He's joking, of course. He knows I can't drive the car.
25 "Barker??" I know that voice! But who …?

Oh! Surprise, surprise! The woman and the boy are Mrs Davidson and Jack! The people from next door.

"Barker! So you're here, too! Great!"

And I can see Sherry now, too. She's coming out from
30 behind the beach huts. What luck for me! "Woof! Woof!"

"A bit of ice cream for you, Barker?"

Mm! I love you, Jack.

---

4 **sandcastle** ['sænd₁kɑːsl] Sandburg • 6 **to lie** [laɪ] liegen • 12 **wave** [weɪv] Welle • 16 **beach hut** ['biːtʃhʌt] Strandhäuschen

"Show us where Ben and the others are, Barker." That's Mrs Davidson. "Then we can all be together."

• • •

That's funny. My pets aren't here! I can't understand it. Mum's beach bag is still here on the sand. And all the towels. The picnic things, too. And Lisa's magazine. But no 5 pets.

"Where are they all, Barker?"

No idea. I can't understand it.

"Well, let's sit down on the sand and wait for them." That's Mrs Davidson. 10

Yes, why not? Jack and his mum can sit and wait. And I can play with Sherry! "Woof!" Come on, Sherry! Chase me round the sandcastle!

• • •

"Look, Dad, there he is!" It's Lisa's voice. "Mum! Ben! Jade! He's back!" 15

Lisa is hugging me now. What a fuss! Don't ask me why.

"Barker! Where were you? We were so worried!"

Worried? Why?

"Don't do that again, Barker." That's Dad. "We get worried if you go off alone." 20

They needn't get worried. After all, I'm not a baby!

"Oh! My poor sandcastle! Barker, you bad dog!" That's Jade. She's angry, I can see that. Now I'm really in the doghouse … Sorry, Jade!

• • •

Now everything is OK again. Finally! My pets are sharing 25 the picnic things with Jack and his mum. And Sherry and I are sitting in the middle. Great!

---

5 **towel** [taʊəl] Handtuch • 16 **to hug** [hʌg] umarmen • 16 **What a fuss!**
[wɒt ə 'fʌs] Was für ein Theater! • 17 **were** [wɜ:] warst/waren • 17 **worried**
['wʌrɪd] besorgt, beunruhigt • 22 **poor** [pʊə] arm • 23 **to be in the doghouse**
[bi: ɪn ðə 'dɒghaʊs] in Ungnade gefallen sein • 25 **to share** [ʃeə] teilen

6 Bonfire Night

There's a long box in Ben's room. Under his bed. And I know what's in it. Fireworks! It's November the Fifth today. And that means it's Bonfire Night tonight. There's a big party every year on Bonfire Night. This time it's at my
5 house. In the garden, that is. I love parties! I'm so excited!

• • •

"Barker! Come away from the bonfire! That's right, Barker. Sit! Be a good dog. Now here's a sausage-roll for you."

Ah, thank you, Lisa! I love sausage-rolls.

We're in the garden. Everybody is here. All my pets, of
10 course. All Lisa's friends, too. Emma and her older sister, Nasreen. Terry and Sam. Some of Ben's friends, too. Jack Davidson from next door is here, of course. And lots of parents, too.

There's a very big bonfire this year. You can't go really
15 near it, because it's so hot! Dad and Mrs Davidson are looking after the bonfire. Ben and Jack are helping them. I'm running round the bonfire again. Lisa doesn't like that, I know. She thinks it's dangerous. But I'm OK.

Now Mum is bringing something to eat. Mm! Let's see
20 what it is.

"Hot jacket potatoes! Who wants a hot potato? Jack?"

"Oh, great! Thanks, Mrs Taylor."

Yuk! I don't like potatoes. Oh well, never mind. Maybe I can play with Sherry. But wait a moment … Where *is*
25 Sherry? I can't see her. She isn't with Jack.

"Hi, Barker!" Jack is patting me on the head. "You're looking for Sherry, right? Well, she's at home." At home? On Bonfire Night? Doesn't she like parties? "She doesn't like fireworks, you see, Barker. She hates all the loud bangs."

---

bonfire ['bɒnfaɪə] Freudenfeuer • **2 firework** ['faɪəwɜːk] Feuerwerkskörper •
7 **sausage-roll** [ˌsɒsidʒ'rəʊl] *Würstchen in Blätterteig* • 16 **to look after sth** [lʊk
'ɑːftə ˌsʌmθiŋ] auf etw. aufpassen • 18 **dangerous** ['deɪndʒərəs] gefährlich •
21 **jacket potato** [ˌdʒækɪt pə'teɪtəʊ] Folien-/Ofenkartoffel • 29 **to hate** [heɪt] hassen

Oh! I understand. Well, never mind. I can go and see what Mr Brook and Emma are doing. They're getting the fireworks ready. – Yes, there they are! Terry and Sam are with them. I can sit and watch.

• • •

The 'quiet' fireworks always come first. I like them a lot. 5
They look great! 'Golden Rain' is my favourite. It's Jade's favourite, too.

"Again! Golden Rain again! Please, Emma! Please, Mr Brook!"

"Sorry, Jade. That's the last Golden Rain this year! Now 10
it's time for the crackers."

Crackers make big bangs. Very big bangs. They don't scare me really. But I understand how Sherry feels about them. Oh! Jack and Ben have got a box of 'Jumping Jacks', too. Help! They're awful things! I must go back a bit. 15

Bang! – Bang! – Bang!

"Hey, Ben! Jack! Watch out!"

11 **cracker** [ˈkrækə] Knaller • 14 **'Jumping Jack'** [ˈdʒʌmpɪŋˌdʒæk] Knallfrosch •
17 **Watch out!** [wɒtʃ ˈaʊt] Pass auf!

19

"Aah!"

Too late! A Jumping Jack is in Jack's trousers now. Yes! Inside the trouser leg!

"Help!!"

5 "Jack! Jack! Are you OK?" Everybody wants to help. But they don't know how!

Now Jack is the Jumping Jack! He's jumping up and down – and shouting! But it's OK. The firework is out now. And Jack is wearing wellies. So his leg is OK, I think.

10 But nobody wants the other crackers now. Mrs Davidson is with Jack. And Jade is crying. No wonder! – Oh, she's OK again now. Ben is giving her a sparkler. She likes that.

"Mr Taylor! Can we have the rockets now?"

"OK, Emma. Ready in a minute!"

15 Rockets are a bit boring. That's what I think, anyway. Just bangs and bits of colour in the sky. Silly, really. Everybody is watching them, of course – But I'm not. I'm looking for that plate with the sausage-rolls. Where can it be?

Ah! Here it is! There are two sausage-rolls still on the
20 plate. That's good – one for me and one for Sherry. So I can eat one now, and I can take one in my mouth for Sherry. If I go through that gap in the fence, I can get to her house. Yes! That's a good idea. I can do that when the party's over. I can bark a bit, and wait outside until she comes. She likes
25 sausage-rolls. Well, I think she does, anyway. And I like her!

7   A special day

Sherry and I are best friends now. She often takes Jack to the park when I take Lisa or Ben. So we play there together a lot. She's only two, so she still has a lot to learn. At the moment I'm teaching her to count. I'm trying, anyway.

---

11 **to cry** [kraɪ] weinen • 12 **sparkler** ['spɑːklə] Wunderkerze • 13 **rocket** ['rɒkɪt] Rakete • 16 **in the sky** [ɪn ðə skaɪ] am Himmel • 22 **gap** [gæp] Lücke • 24 **until** [ən'tɪl] bis • 29 **to teach** [tiːtʃ] beibringen, belehren

There's a pond in the park, you see. With ducks on it. Sometimes we look at the ducks and I count them. You know: "One – two – three – lots!" But Sherry can't count like that yet. She gets mixed up after two.

• • •

It's Sunday again. No picnic today. But it's raining anyway, 5 and my pets don't like to go out much in wet weather. Everybody is at home. And guess what! Lisa says today is a very special day for me. There's another party at our house this afternoon. Just for me! She says it's a surprise. Well! How can a party be a surprise? It's a puzzle. 10

• • •

Half past three. There are tea things on the table. Scones and chocolate cake. Mm! Are they for me?

I can hear voices outside. Who can it be? Now I'm running into the hall. Lisa, Ben and Jade are already there, and Ben is just opening the door. 15

"Hello, everybody! Hi, Barker!" It's Jack.

"Hi, Jack! Hello, Mrs Davidson. Come in!"

Mum and Dad are in the hall, too, now.

"Well, where's Sherry, then?" Dad is speaking to Mrs Davidson and Jack. 20

"Here she is!" Mrs Davidson is looking behind her. "Come in, Sherry! Don't be shy, dear!"

And now I can see Sherry. She's coming in behind the others. That's great.

• • •

Sherry and I are in the living room now. Mrs Davidson 25 is with us. All the others are in the dining room – with the door closed. There they are – with all the scones and

---

1 **duck** [dʌk] Ente • 4 **to get mixed up** [get ˌmɪkst ˈʌp] durcheinander kommen •
11 **scone** [skɒn] *kleines, brötchenartiges Gebäck* • 22 **shy** [ʃaɪ] schüchtern •
27 **closed** [kləʊzd] geschlossen, zu

chocolate cake! They're all talking and laughing – I can hear them. And I'm so hungry!

Never mind. Sherry is here, and she wants to play with me, of course. That's nice.

5   Maybe I can show Sherry my old ball. Yes! I can push it to her with my nose. Then we can play with it together. – Oh, good – she likes that!

Now we're running round the sofa. Sherry is really fast! Now I'm chasing her round the room. That's nice. And now
10 she's chasing me! Everything is great fun. Sherry knows a lot of good games – and it's really nice to be together. I'm not thinking about the scones and the chocolate cake now. A party – without food? Funny – but nice!

• • •

Half past eight. Now Sherry and I are sitting in the dining
15 room with all our pets. We are the centre of attention. Jack

---

5 to push [pʊʃ] schieben • **15 to be the centre of attention** [bi: ðə ˈsentər əv əˌtenʃn] im Mittelpunkt stehen

is stroking Sherry. And Lisa is stroking me! Everybody is happy. And the best thing is: There are two pieces of chocolate cake left! Yes! One for me and one for Sherry.

• • •

Now it's getting late. Sherry and her pets must go home. We're at the door, and everybody is saying goodbye. Sherry 5 is wagging her tail. Jack is patting me on the head.

"Good night, everybody." That's Mrs Davidson. "And thanks for the little party."

And they're off.

Soon Lisa is in bed. I'm near her, of course. It's time to 10 say good night.

"OK, Barker?"

Yes, I'm OK. I'm tired, and I think Lisa must be tired, too. Good night, Lisa. And thanks for another happy day!

8   Christmas Day

"Happy Christmas, Barker! Hey, Barker, wake up! Good 15 dog!"

What's going on? Why is Lisa awake so early? Oh yes, now I know. Of course! It's Christmas Day. She's always awake very early on Christmas Day. Too early, I think …

"Look, Barker, here's my Christmas stocking! Let's go 20 to Jade's room. Then we can open our presents together. Come on!"

Jade can't be awake so very early, I'm sure. But she is! And Ben is there, too – he's sitting on her bed. Now, that's a big surprise! Ben usually likes to sleep so long. 25

"Happy Christmas, Lisa!" That's Ben. "Hey, Barker, it's Christmas Day!"

---

3 **left** [left] *hier:* übrig •17 **What's going on?** [ˌwɒts ˈgəʊɪŋ ˈɒn] Was ist los? •
20 **stocking** [ˈstɒkɪŋ] Strumpf • 22 **Come on!** [kʌm ˈɒn] Komm! Los! • 23 **sure**
[ʃɔː; ʃʊə] sicher

I know that. He needn't tell me! How silly does he think I am?

"Look, Lisa!" That's Jade. "New clothes for my doll! And a puzzle."

5 "Great, Jade! And look what I've got – a new computer game! *Ghost train*!"

"Let me see." That's Ben again. "Hey, it looks really good. – Now let's see what's in my stocking. Look, Barker, Christmas presents!"

10 How boring! No food – except sweets. (I don't like sweets much. Chocolate is nicer.) And nothing with a nice smell! Just books, games, DVDs and silly things like that. Ah, well! I can just lie here on Jade's bed and sleep a bit … Good that Mum can't see me here! The old pets aren't awake yet.

15 Their bedroom door is closed!

• • •

It's eleven o'clock now. I'm in my bed in the kitchen. My Christmas present from my pets is very nice. It's a rubber bone – with a strong smell of chocolate! And it tastes of chocolate, too! I've got it in my bed here now. I've got

20 another present, too – from Lisa. It's a new comb. Lisa uses it on my coat, and I like that a lot! It feels really good. And Lisa says it makes my coat nice and silky, too.

Well, Lisa is at church now with Dad and Jade. I can't go into churches. (Sometimes my pets go into a church

25 when we go on a trip. They always leave me outside the door. Churches are a 'no-no' for dogs, you see. Don't ask me why.) Anyway, it's very nice here in the kitchen today. Mum and Ben are making the Christmas dinner. Turkey! The smell in the kitchen is great!

---

3 doll [dɒl] Puppe • **10 except** [ɪk'sept] außer • **20 comb** [kəʊm] Kamm •
22 silky ['sɪlki] seidig • **23 at church** [ət 'tʃɜːtʃ] in der Kirche • **28 turkey** ['tɜːki]
Truthahn

And guess what! There's a special Christmas menu for me today! (Lisa's idea, of course. That girl is a wonder!) This is it:

First course: Cornflake and popcorn special. (That's cornflakes and bits of popcorn, on a plate with little bits 5 of dog biscuit.)

Second course: Christmas turkey. (Yes! Really big bits of turkey. Without bones, of course. Turkey bones are too small for dogs. Lisa knows that.)

Third course: Christmas pudding. (Well, maybe I like it. 10 I'm not sure yet …)

Last course: Cheese and biscuits. (Great! Real English cheese, and real pets' biscuits!)

• • •

It's half past four. We're in the living room now. The lights on the Christmas tree are on. It looks very nice. 15

The TV is on, too. Not so interesting for me, of course. Well, maybe we can play our game! Here I am, in front of the TV. Come on, then, everybody! Throw things at me!

But nothing is happening. Why not? That's funny. They're all here! Or are they? 20

Oh, just look at that! Mum and Dad are asleep in their armchairs! And Lisa and Ben? Where can they be? Oh, they're upstairs now. They're trying out Lisa's new computer game. I can hear it. Boring! And Jade? Oh, there she is. She's doing her new puzzle. 25

Well, nobody wants to play with me. I can see that. Nobody wants to go out. But I've got my nice new chocolate bone. That's lucky! And there's nobody on the sofa just now … Ah! Great! This is what I call a really happy Christmas! 30

---

1 **menu** ['menjuː] Menü • 4 **course** [kɔːs] *hier:* Gang • 10 **Christmas pudding** [ˌkrɪsməs'pʊdiŋ] *kuchenartige Nachspeise* • 12 **biscuit** ['bɪskɪt] Keks, Kräcker • 14 **light** [laɪt] Licht • 22 **armchair** ['ɑːmtʃeə] Sessel

9 An afternoon with Ben and Jade

Christmas is over. The Christmas tree is still in the living room. But nobody really looks at it now! Anyway, it's Thursday today. The Jazz Café is always closed on Thursday afternoons, so I'm usually at home then. Lisa isn't here this
5 afternoon. She's in town with Mum. I hope they remember to buy my favourite dog biscuits …

It's very quiet. Dad is working, I think. Ben and Jade are upstairs. But maybe they have got time for me. – Oh yes, they're coming down now! Ah, Ben is getting my lead –
10 that's good.

"Come here, Barker! We're going out!"

• • •

It's very cold outside today. But my coat is nice and warm, of course, so that's OK. We're on the way to the park now.
15 Ben is holding my lead, and Jade is talking to me. I like that! "Maybe Sherry is in the park today, Barker. Maybe she's there with Jack!"

Yes, maybe. But I'm not thinking about Sherry. I can see another dog now – a poodle! I don't know him yet. Come
20 on, Ben, let's go and say hello.

"Woof! Woof!"

"Don't pull on the lead like that, Barker! – Oh well, OK then. Let's say hello to that poodle over there."

The poodle can see us now. He's wagging his tail – that's
25 good. Here he comes. – Hello, little poodle!

But oh no – just look at him. He's got a jacket on! Yes, a jacket! How silly. It's cold today, I know that. But I think dogs look really silly in jackets.

5 **to hope** [həʊp] hoffen • 15 **to hold** [həʊld] halten • 22 **to pull** [pʊl] ziehen • 26 **jacket** [ˈdʒækɪt] Jacke

"Woof! Woof!"

Well, he's friendly, anyway. Maybe he's OK.

• • •

Ben knows a lot of tricks from me. When I bring him a stick, he throws it for me. That's always fun. We're in the park now, and I've got a nice big stick. – Here, Ben! Throw!　5

Oh, great! I'm running after the stick now. It's near the pond. Yes, there it is. I've got it in my mouth again now.

"Hey, there's Barker! Hello, Barker! Is Lisa with you?"

Who's that? Oh, it's Sam Spencer. Lisa's friend! With Phil, his cousin from London. They're near the pond. I must go　10 to them and say hello.

"Oh, look, there's Ben! And Jade! – Hello, you two. We're just playing with Phil's Christmas present. Come and look!"

Phil has got a toy car. It's a police car, I think.　15

"Look, Ben. It's got remote control!"

"Hey, that's great! Can I try it, too, Phil?"

"Yeah, OK. Here's the remote."

It's a nice little car. It can go right or left – and it can go backwards, too. I don't know how it works, but it really is　20 very clever. Now Jade wants to try it, too.

"*Please*, Phil! Let me try! I can do it!"

"Well, OK, Jade. But be careful with it."

Now Jade has got the remote. The car is driving down the path near the pond.　25

"Careful, Jade. Not too near the pond!"

"OK, Phil."

"Woof! Woof!! Woof!!!"

Now what's going on? Oh – it's that funny little poodle with the jacket on. He's running after Phil's car. Oh no!　30

"Jade! Give me the remote! Careful! Don't –"

---

4 stick [stɪk] Stock • **15 police** [pə'liːs] Polizei • **16 remote (control)** [rɪˌməʊt kən'trəʊl] Fernbedienung • **20 backwards** ['bækwədz] rückwärts • **23 to be careful** [biː 'keəfl] aufpassen, vorsichtig sein • **25 path** [pɑːθ] Weg

But Phil is too late. The little car is going straight to the pond. Now …!

There's no splash. That's funny. – Oh, I see now – the car isn't in the pond, it's on it! Yes! There's ice on the pond
5 today!

"Hey, it's on the ice. It's OK! Look, Phil. Look what I can do!"

Jade has still got the remote. But Phil wants it back.

"Come on, Jade. We must get the car off the ice."

10 "But it's fun on the ice, Phil. Watch!"

The car is very fast on the ice. Everybody is watching it now. The poodle is watching it, too. He's standing by the pond and barking. I think he's scared of the ice! Anyway, he isn't running after the car now.

15 Now Sam has got the remote.

"Watch, everybody! There it goes! Wow! – Oh! Wait a minute – I can't start it now. Oh no – what's going on?"

"Give me the remote, Sam. Don't be a pain – it's *my* car!"

"OK, Phil. Sorry! Here you are."

20 But the car doesn't work now. Phil can't start it.

"Maybe it's the batteries, Phil." That's Ben.

"Oh yeah, maybe it is. I think you're right, Ben. Maybe it needs a new battery."

"Well, let's pick it up and go home then." That's Jade.
25 "We've got batteries at home!"

"But Jade! You can't – "

Crack! The ice on the pond is thin here. Jade's shoes are very wet now. Her trousers, too.

"Oh no!" That's Phil. "What can we do? My car is in the
30 middle of the pond – and we can't get it!"

---

3 **There's no splash.** [ðeəz nəʊ ˈsplæʃ] Es platscht nicht. • 27 **Crack!** [kræk] Knack! • 27 **thin** [θɪn] dünn

Phil is upset. No wonder! I feel sorry for him. But what can I do? Nothing! But wait … Maybe I can try …

"Hey, Barker! Don't go on the ice – it's too thin! Barker, come here!"

But I'm not listening to Ben. I'm on the ice now. And I'm OK! I'm very careful, of course. And I must say, it isn't easy! My legs feel a bit funny on the ice … Oops! I'm slipping a bit now!

"Oh, Barker! Careful!"

"Look, Ben!" That's Jade's voice. "He's got Phil's car in his mouth! He's got it! He's got it!"

"Wow! That's great! Good dog, Barker! But careful now … That's right – not too fast!"

• • •

---

1 **upset** [ʌp'set] verärgert, unglücklich, bestürzt • **7 to slip** [slɪp] (aus)rutschen

I am the centre of attention. We are all in the kitchen at the Spencers' house in Wendover Road. (Not that silly poodle, of course. He isn't with us!) I'm a bit cold and wet. But that's OK. Everybody is stroking me. I'm wagging my tail
5 all the time, I'm so happy!

Sam's grandma is cooking sausages. And Sam says there are two sausages for me!

"How many sausages for you, Barker?"

"Woof! Woof!"

10 "That's right. 'Woof woof' is 'two'. Clever dog. – Hey, Ben! Jade! He can count!"

"We know that already, Sam." Jade is speaking. "Barker is a superdog!"

Thank you, Jade!

10 More surprises

15 It's Friday afternoon. Mum and I are back from the Jazz Café. It's too late to go to the park. But never mind. It's nice and warm here in Lisa's room. She's smiling at me now and she looks excited.

"Hey, Barker! Jack and his mum want to see us this
20 evening. At their house. All of us. That means you can come, too! OK?"

Of course it's OK. I want to see Sherry again! Because I don't often see her these days. She never goes to the park now. Maybe she doesn't like the cold weather. I don't know.

• • •

25 Well, here we are at Sherry's house now. Mrs Davidson is at the door. But I don't see Sherry. Where can she be?

"Come in, everybody! Great to see you all. Give me your jackets, OK?"

---

6 to cook [kʊk] *hier:* braten • **24 weather** [ˈweðə] Wetter

Now Jack is patting me on the head. "Hello, Barker! Good dog! We've got a little surprise for you today. Come with me into the kitchen. I want to show you something."

A surprise? In the kitchen? How exciting! What can it be? Hot sausage-rolls? Chocolate cake? 5

• • •

Everybody is in the kitchen now. But there's no food. Mrs Davidson is making tea for Mum and Dad. Lisa, Ben and Jade are sitting on the floor with Jack.

"Oh! Aren't they sweet!" That's Lisa.

"Look, Lisa. Their eyes are still closed!" That's Jade. 10

"How old are they, Jack?" That's Ben.

"They're just five days old. – Hey, Barker, come and look at Sherry's puppies!"

Puppies? I can't believe it! But it's true. There are three of them. They're in a special box in a corner of the kitchen. 15 Sherry is with them.

But I want to play with Sherry, of course. I'm looking at her and I'm barking now.

"Woof! Woof!" Come and play with me, Sherry!

But Sherry isn't looking at me. She's only interested in 20 the puppies. How silly! I can't understand it.

"Don't be upset, Barker!" Lisa is stroking me. "Sherry hasn't got time for you at the moment. She's a mum now, you see. So her puppies come first. OK, Barker?"

No, it isn't OK. I really *am* upset now. How can Sherry 25 be so silly?

"Come here, Barker." Ben is talking to me now. "We've got *another* surprise for you. Are you listening?"

Of course I'm listening. What a silly question!

"Well, you're a superdog, Barker. We know *that*! But that 30 isn't all. You aren't just a superdog. You're also a super*dad*! Sherry's puppies are your puppies, too!"

---

13 **puppy** ['pʌpi] Welpe • 14 **true** [truː] wahr • 15 **corner** ['kɔːnə] Ecke

My puppies? How funny! Well!! – So now *I'm* the centre of attention again! That's great. Wow!

"Biscuits for you, Barker?" That's Jack. "Have some from this new packet. They're Sherry's favourite food."

5   Mmm! It's great to be a superdad!

• • •

Sherry and I are best friends again. She's still a mum, of course. But I sometimes go through the gap in the fence
10 when she's outside in their garden. Then we can be together a bit. She tells me a lot about the puppies. Their names are Timmy, Bobby and Bella.

Lisa says they're seven weeks old now. And that means they must go to new homes soon. Yes! They can't stay with Sherry and her pets. Jack and his mum don't want four dogs in the family! But it's hard for Sherry. She doesn't
15 want to say goodbye to the puppies, of course. So she's a bit upset today.

• • •

The puppies have all got new homes now. Finally! Timmy
20 and Bobby are together. Their new pets live in a house in London. I hope it's nice for them there. Bella's new home is in Wendover Road.

"With Mr and Mrs Carter!" Lisa is telling me all about it. "Mrs Carter is my German teacher. She *loves* Bella! And
25 guess what! She says 'Bella' sounds like 'bellen' in German – so the name is a bit like 'Barker' in English! Isn't that funny?"

German? What's that? I don't understand! But I hope Bella is happy with the Carters. Some dogs have an awful
30 time with their pets. Sherry and I are lucky.

---

25 to sound [saʊnd] klingen, sich anhören

So life is back to normal again in Pond Road. Sherry has time for me again. The days are warmer now, and we often play together in the park.

Oh, and guess what! Sherry is a superdog, too. She can count to three now! She says, if you've got three puppies, you soon learn to count them. Easy! You just say: 'One! Two! And another!' 5

Well, I must say goodbye now. It's Saturday evening, and all my pets are at home. We're in the living room. They're all watching TV. And I'm sitting – you know where! 10

Ouch!! A rubber on the back of my head! – Aah! A shoe! – Oww!!! Another shoe! – A cushion!

"It's a dog's life!" Dad sometimes says that when things get on top of him. Now I think maybe I understand what he means ... 15

---

12 **cushion** ['kʊʃn] (Sofa-)Kissen • 13 **when things get on top of him**
[wen ˌθɪŋz get ɒn 'tɒp əv hɪm] wenn ihm alles zu viel wird

Things to do and talk about

1 Barker and his life

From Chapter 3 'Later in the day':

1. Barker and his family live in … Road.   2. Barker's favourite pet is …   3. But sometimes little … gives him his food.   4. … doesn't like to see him on Lisa's bed! 5. … hasn't always got time for Barker.   6. …, the cat, runs away when he barks.   7. Barker has an important job at the … Café.   8. His favourite food is '… Bark-a-Lot'.

2 Let's play a game: 'Find the pairs'

From Chapter 5 'A day by the sea':

- *Make a list of twenty-five things from* Barker's World. *Examples: rabbit, plate, fish, cat, house, ice-cream …*
- *Now make 50 cards.*
- *Draw pictures of these things on 25 cards.*
- *Write the names of the things on the other 25 cards.*
- *Put all the cards on the table – so you can't see the words and pictures.*
- *Now – can you find the pairs?*
- *You can play the game with two or more players.*

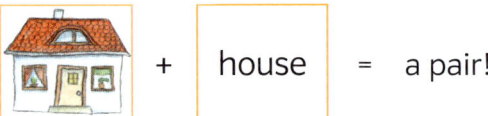 + house = a pair!

Example:
Sam takes two cards. If they make a pair, he can keep the cards. Then it's his turn again.
But if they don't make a pair, he must put them back on the table. Then it's the next player's turn.
The player with most cards at the end wins.

---

chapter ['tʃæptər] Kapitel • **most** [məʊst] die meisten

3 Things to eat

From Chapter 6 'Bonfire Night':

a) *What does Barker like to eat?*
   Make a list. How many things can
   you think of? Talk about him – and
   what he likes – or doesn't like.

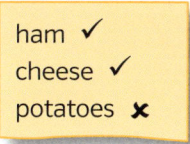

ham ✔
cheese ✔
potatoes ✘

"Barker likes ham."
"Yes, he does. And he likes cheese, too."
"But he doesn't like …"

b) *Do you like the things on the list? And what about*
   your friends?

"I like cheese. Do you like it, too?"
"Yes, I do." / "No, I don't."
"I don't like potatoes. Do you like them?"
"Yes, I do." / "Well, I don't like jacket potatoes much.
But I love crisps!"

c) *Now you can play a game. Here's an example:*

Lisa: My dog likes popcorn.
Emma: My dog likes popcorn and jacket potatoes.
Sam: My dog likes popcorn, jacket potatoes and
        chocolate.
Terry: My dog likes popcorn, jacket potatoes,
        chocolate and …

4 How do they feel?

From Chapter 7 'A special day':

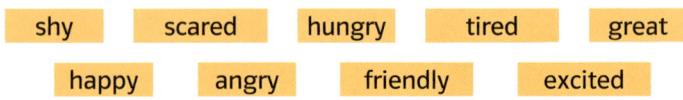

shy	scared	hungry	tired	great

happy	angry	friendly	excited

a) *How does Barker feel …*

1. … when people stroke him? – He feels happy.
2. … when people come into the Jazz Café?
3. … when he sees the picnic things?
4. … when he finds he can swim?
5. … when he knows the Bonfire Night party is at his house?
6. … after the surprise party with Sherry?
7. … when cats come into his garden?

b) *How does Sherry feel …*

1. … on Bonfire Night?
2. … when she comes to the surprise party at the Taylors' house?

5 Barker – and your pets

From Chapter 8 'Christmas Day':

Talk about Barker and your pets.
Example: 1. Barker sleeps on Lisa's bed.
– Our dog never sleeps on my bed.
– My aunt's dogs sleep on her bed, too.
– Our cat sometimes sleeps on the sofa.

2. Barker loves trips in the car.
3. He likes to chase rabbits.
4. He often sits in front of the TV.
5. He likes fireworks / isn't scared of fireworks.
6. He likes to be the centre of attention.

Have you got more ideas? Go on if you can.

6 A birthday cake for dogs

From Chapter 8 'Christmas Day':

*You can make this cake for your dog's birthday.
It's very easy!*

What you need:

- Half a pound of dog biscuits
- Little bits of ham or sausage
- One egg
- A small packet of cream cheese.

Crush the dog biscuits. (You can put them in a
strong plastic bag and crush them with a rolling pin.)

Mix the cream cheese with the egg.

Mix everything together. (Put a little milk in, too,
if you need it.)

Now press the mixture into a small bowl.

Leave it for two or three hours.

Then turn the cake out on a plate. Ready!

*Remember! Dogs don't like candles on their cakes!
But you can sing "Happy birthday", of course!*

half a pound [hɑːf ə 'paʊnd] ein halbes Pfund • **egg** [eg] Ei • **cream cheese**
[kriːm'tʃiːz] Frischkäse • **to crush** [krʌʃ] zerkleinern • **rolling pin** ['rəʊlɪŋˌpɪn]
Nudelholz • **to mix** [mɪks] mischen • **to press** [pres] drücken • **mixture** ['mɪkstʃə]
Mischung, Teig • **to turn (a cake) out** [tɜːn ə keɪk 'aʊt] (einen Kuchen) stürzen

7 Barker and his family and friends: a puzzle

From Chapter 10 'More surprises':

Across →

1. Sue Taylor and her helper make … the food at the Jazz Café.
3. Where … the Taylors live? – In Pond Road.
5. Lisa … Barker's favourite pet.
8. Barker has a very important … at the Jazz Café.
10. Barker is usually awake … six o'clock.
11. Yuk! Barker doesn't like to have sand in his mouth and …
12. Barker has got a small bed in the …
14. At home, Barker thinks he is the …

16. The Taylors often go for … in the car on Sundays.
17. Barker is four, but Sherry is only …
20. Timmy, Bobby and Bella are Sherry's …
22. Barker sometimes calls Mum and Dad 'the old …'!
24. Barker and Sherry aren't poodles. They're both …
27. At the Jazz Café Barker is a great …
28. Phil's police car has got … control.

Down ↓

2. When Barker wakes Lisa up, he … her face.
3. Barker is wet and … when he comes out of the stream.
4. Barker's Christmas present is a rubber …
6. TV is boring for Barker. There are only pictures, no …!
7. This animal lives in a hole.
9. There's a big … in the Taylors' garden on November 5th.
13. Jacket potatoes are best when they're …
15. When Barker wants to see Sherry, he can go through a … in the fence.
18. Barker likes to look … of the car window.
19. When people come into the Jazz Café, Barker never jumps …
21. The sausage-rolls are on a …
22. Phil's car first drives down the … near the pond, then it goes on the ice.
23. Careful on the ice, Barker! Don't …!
25. Barker always likes to … the centre of attention, of course.
26. Where is Sherry on Bonfire Night? Barker can't … her.

Solutions

Before you read
Individual answers

Things to do and talk about

1 Barker and his life
1. Pond; 2. Lisa; 3. Jade; 4. Mum/Sue Taylor; 5. Ben;
6. Tiger; 7. Jazz; 8. Beef

2 Let's play a game: 'Find the pairs'
No solutions (game)

3 Things to eat
a) ham; cheese; dog biscuits; Chicken Bark-a-Lot; Beef Bark-a-Lot;
popcorn; fish; ice cream; sausage rolls; NOT potatoes
(from '7 A special day': scones; chocolate cake;
from '8 Christmas Day': chocolate; NOT sweets; turkey;
cornflakes; Christmas Pudding (maybe!); (pets') biscuits;
from '9 An afternoon with Ben and Jade': sausages)

b) *Individual answers*

c) *No solutions (game)*

4 How do they feel?
a) 1. happy; 2. friendly; 3. hungry; 4. great;
   5. excited; 6. tired; 7. angry
b) 1. scared; 2. shy

5 Barker – and your pets
Ideas:
2. Our dog loves trips in the car, too; My friend's dog doesn't
   like trips in the car; Our dog/cat always sleeps when he/she is
   in the car with us …
3. Our dog likes to chase cats; There are no rabbits where
   we live …